Turn It Down!

By Susan Blackaby

CELEBRATION PRESS

Pearson Learning Group

The following people from **Pearson Learning Group**
have contributed to the development of this product:

Joan Mazzeo, Dorothea Fox **Design** | **Editorial** Leslie Feierstone Barna, Cindy Kane
Christine Fleming **Marketing** | **Publishing Operations** Jennifer Van Der Heide
Production Laura Benford-Sullivan
Content Area Consultant Dr. Amy Rabb-Liu and Dr. Charles Liu

The following people from **DK** have
contributed to the development of this product:

Art Director Rachael Foster

Martin Wilson **Managing Art Editor** | **Managing Editor** Marie Greenwood
Nick Harris, Jane Tetzlaff **Design** | **Editorial** Marian Broderick, Jennie Morris
Diana Morris, Pernilla Pearce **Picture Research** | **Production** Gordana Simakovic
Richard Czapnik, Andy Smith **Cover Design** | **DTP** David McDonald
Consultant David Glover

Dorling Kindersley would like to thank: Shirley Cachia and Rose Horridge in the DK Picture Library; Andy Crawford for new photography; Cynthia Frazer, Helen McFarland, Carlo Ortun, and Mariana Sonnenberg for additional picture research; Ian Midson for additional design work; Johnny Pau for additional cover design work; and models Kayude Adeniran, Kwade Davis, and Ayshe Khan.

Picture Credits: Action Images: Michael Regan 11. Aearo Ltd: 17tr, 17cra, 17br, 17cfr. Alamy Images: Bipinchandra Mistry 29b; Ian Patrick 21t. Corbis: Peter Beck 27b; Bruce Burkhardt 7r; David Butow 16; Pablo Corral V 22cr; Firefly Productions 19br; George Hall 22tr; Paul Hardy 6crb; Roy Morsch 8tr;Jose Luis Pelaez, Inc. 5clb; PictureNet 7clb; Reg Charity 29cfl; RNT Productions 29tl; Alan Schein Photography 4-5,b; Charlie Samuels 25; Chuck Savage 6cb; Schenectady Museum; Hall of Electrical History Foundation 23br; Ariel Skelley 20; Richard Hamilton Smith 22br; Bob Winsett 30. DK Images: Geoff Brightling 13b; Denoyer-Geppert Intl. 13b; Stephen Oliver 21b. Getty Images: The Image Bank /John William Banagan 4cl. Masterfile UK: Pierre Tremblay 6cbl. NASA: 10. NSCA: Elaine Cripps 26. Photolibrary.com: Wodonga Regional Health Service 27tr. Redferns: Paul Bergen/Redferns 14-15. Reuters: Alexandra Winkler 24bl. Royalty Free Images: Corbis 22acr, 23clb, 28. Science Photo Library: Susumu Nishinaga 13tr. Cover: Corbis: Bruce Burkhardt front c; Alan Schein Photography front c background. ImageState/Pictor: front cr. NSCA: Elaine Cripps back.

All other images: ⬛ Dorling Kindersley © 2005. For further information see www.dkimages.com

ISBN: 0-7652-5237-6

Color reproduction by Colourscan, Singapore
Printed in the United States of America
6 7 8 9 10   08 07 06

1-800-321-3106
www.pearsonlearning.com

Contents

Turn It Down!

Listen. Do you hear something? Chances are, the answer is yes. Sound is all around us. In fact, in many places, complete quiet can be hard to find.

Many of the sounds we hear around us are unwanted sounds, or **noise**. In urban areas, noise comes mostly from traffic, construction, and people. Noise in rural areas can come from farm equipment, passing trains, and low-flying planes.

Both rural areas (left) and cities (below) experience **noise pollution**.

The problem is that many people do not realize that noise can have serious negative effects. Of course, noise can be irritating. More than that, excessive noise, called noise pollution, harms the environment, just like trash and chemicals do. Loud or prolonged noise can damage your hearing and even threaten your health. In this book, you will learn more about the negative effects of excessive noise and about the precautions you can take to guard against its dangers. You will see that protecting yourself from too much noise is a sound decision!

The volume control of a personal stereo is often turned up to a dangerous level.

Sound Versus Noise

No one would argue the importance of sound. Sound helps you to understand the world around you. Some sounds, such as speech, allow you to communicate with others. Other sounds, such as car horns and alarms, are useful as warnings. Still other sounds, such as music, entertain you and help you to relax.

Yet speech, alarms, and music are sometimes considered noise, too. Sound becomes noise when it is unwelcome or unwanted. (In fact, the word *noise* comes from the Latin word *nausea*, which means "seasickness.") What people consider noise is usually determined by time, place, and the mood of the listener. For example, everyday speech is a useful, helpful sound that people depend on in order to communicate. However, in a setting where it bothers others, such as a theater or a library, everyday speech becomes noise.

Are these sounds or noises? It depends on your point of view.

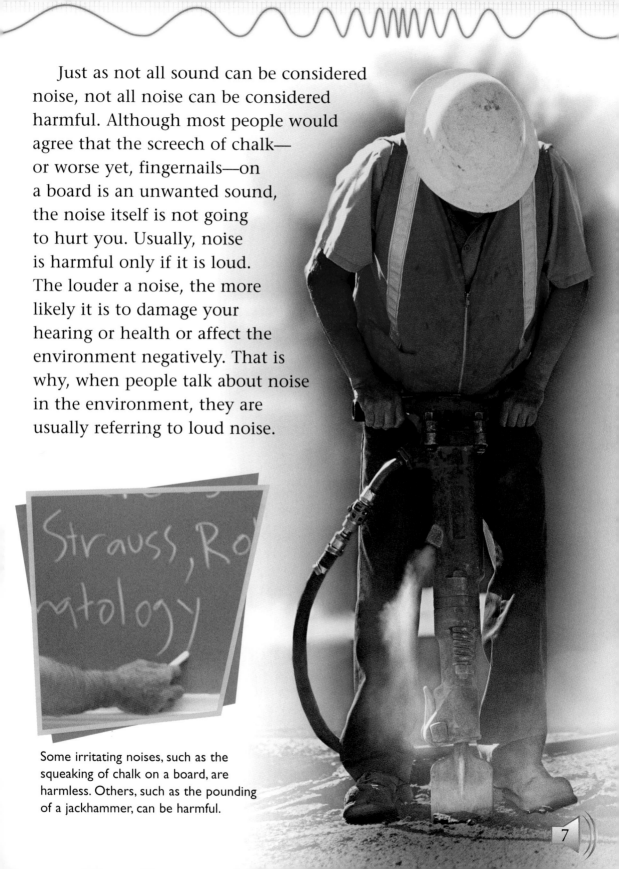

Just as not all sound can be considered noise, not all noise can be considered harmful. Although most people would agree that the screech of chalk— or worse yet, fingernails—on a board is an unwanted sound, the noise itself is not going to hurt you. Usually, noise is harmful only if it is loud. The louder a noise, the more likely it is to damage your hearing or health or affect the environment negatively. That is why, when people talk about noise in the environment, they are usually referring to loud noise.

Some irritating noises, such as the squeaking of chalk on a board, are harmless. Others, such as the pounding of a jackhammer, can be harmful.

How Loud Is Too Loud?

The louder a noise, the more likely it is to damage your hearing. At what point does a noise become too loud? To answer that question, it's important to know a little about how sound works.

Sound waves spread from the source of a noise like ripples in water.

Sound Waves

Sound is produced when an object **vibrates**, or moves back and forth very quickly. This movement also makes the air around the object vibrate. The air transmits the vibrations in the form of **sound waves**. Most of the sounds that people hear travel in the same way that ripples spread out from a pebble thrown into a pond.

How Sound Waves Are Created

Think of how a guitar string vibrates when plucked. The vibration causes air molecules around the string to move. These molecules hit nearby molecules, and those molecules hit molecules near them. The molecules become **compressed**, or squeezed together.

As the vibrating string moves back, it leaves space into which the molecules can spread, separating them again from nearby molecules, which in turn separate from molecules next to them, and so on. The combination of compressing and separating of molecules creates a sound wave that travels away from the vibrating string.

Air molecules vibrate to produce sound when a guitar string is plucked.

Sound waves, although invisible, can be compared to ocean waves. The highest point of the wave is called the **crest**. The lowest point is called the **trough**. Half of the height of a sound wave—the distance between the crest and the trough—is called its **amplitude**. The amplitude determines the intensity, or loudness, of a sound.

The size of a wave's amplitude depends on the degree to which the molecules are being compressed by the vibration. As a rule, the more bunched up the molecules are when they are being compressed, the more energy a sound wave contains and the higher its amplitude. When the molecules are not as compressed, the sound wave has a smaller amplitude and carries less energy.

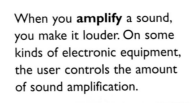

When you **amplify** a sound, you make it louder. On some kinds of electronic equipment, the user controls the amount of sound amplification.

Sound Waves, Energy, and Loudness

Different sounds have differently shaped waves.

crest
low amplitude
trough

This sound contains a small amount of energy. It has a low amplitude and produces a soft sound.

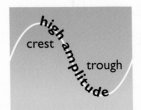

high amplitude
crest
trough

This sound contains a large amount of energy. It has a high amplitude and produces a loud sound.

Measuring Loudness

Units called **decibels** (dB) are used to measure the amplitude, or loudness, of a sound. A soft whisper measures 30 dB; a conversation measures about 60 dB. A prolonged sound of 80 dB is loud enough to cause pain or even damage to the ear.

Surprisingly, quite a few familiar sounds are louder than 80 dB. For example, the movements of a large truck or subway train and the noise from construction sites all exceed this level. Listening to music through stereo headphones can, too. In fact, sound coming through the headphones of the average personal stereo set at medium volume can reach levels of more than 90 dB.

The Decibel Scale	
dB	**EXAMPLE**
0	Softest sound a human can hear
30	Low whispering
40	Quiet bank, living room
50	Refrigerator, far-off traffic
60	Talking, nearby air conditioner
70	Noisy cafeteria, heavy traffic
80	Nearby alarm clock, city traffic
90	Blender, lawn mower, truck traffic
100	Music heard on headphones, chain saw
120	Loud thunderclap, music heard near speakers at a rock concert
140	Airplane, gunshot
180	Rocket launch

Rocket launches are among the loudest sounds humans have ever produced.

Reflection and Absorption

Another way to determine how damaging a loud noise might be is to simply look around a room or an area. Sound waves can be reflected or absorbed as they travel out from their source.

An echo is an example of sound **reflection**. It is caused by sound waves bouncing off a hard surface. Sound reflection makes it possible for you to hear your own voice come back when you yell, "Hello!" in a big empty room.

Think about how noisy a cafeteria can be. The hard plastic furniture, plastic trays, linoleum floor, and smooth walls are all surfaces that reflect sound. On the other hand, soft materials such as draperies, screens, carpets, and upholstered furniture **absorb** sound. These absorbent materials soak up some of the energy of sound waves and decrease noise. Noise-conscious architects and builders often add sound-absorbing features to places in which large numbers of people spend time, such as restaurants and offices. However, these features don't eliminate noise entirely. In many places, loud noise is still a problem.

A racquetball court's smooth walls and floor don't absorb sound well, making the court noisy.

Your Hearing at Risk

Certain kinds of noise can have serious effects on your hearing. A complex chain of events allows us to hear. If just one part of the chain is not working or is damaged, loss of hearing can result. One common cause of ear damage is exposure to loud noises over a long period of time.

Hearing Basics

To fully understand why noise can do so much damage to your hearing, it's important to know how the human ear works. The ear has three parts—the outer, middle, and inner ear. The outer or external part of the ear is called the pinna (or auricle). This flap of skin and cartilage that surrounds the opening of the ear canal works like a funnel to catch and reflect sound waves down into the ear canal.

pinna

The ear canal is a narrow tube that is closed off at one end by the eardrum. Sound waves enter the ear and travel down the canal to the eardrum. The waves make the eardrum vibrate. Tiny bones called ossicles transmit the vibrations to the inner ear.

The cochlea (KOK-lee-uh) is a spiral-shaped structure in the inner ear that contains fluid and thousands of extremely sensitive hair cells. Vibrations move through the fluid inside the cochlea, creating ripples. The ripples cause the fluid to move bundles of hair cells that line the inside of the cochlea. The hair bundles turn the vibrations into nerve impulses that are sent to the brain, where they are interpreted as sound.

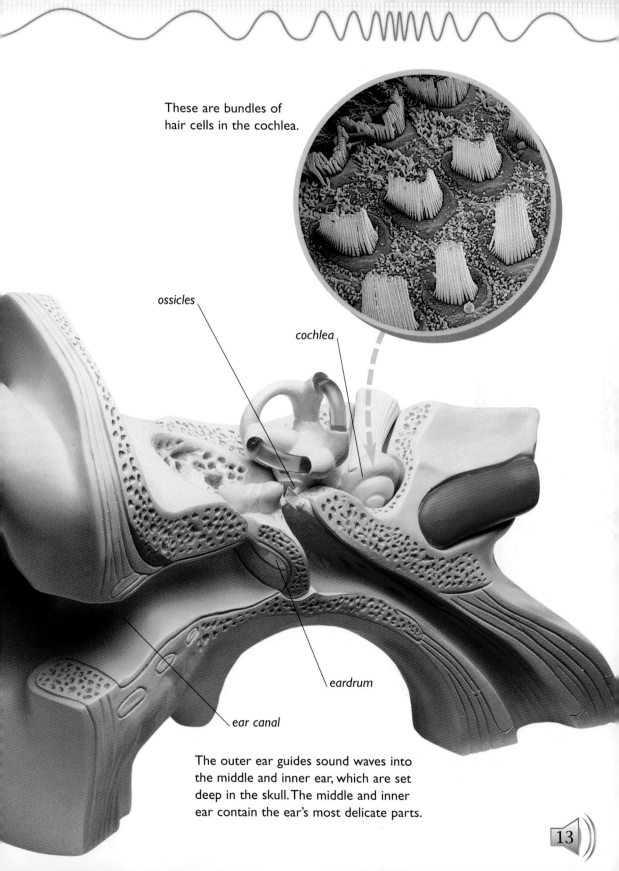

These are bundles of
hair cells in the cochlea.

ossicles

cochlea

eardrum

ear canal

The outer ear guides sound waves into
the middle and inner ear, which are set
deep in the skull. The middle and inner
ear contain the ear's most delicate parts.

Damaging Noise

Several factors can affect the ability of the ear to work correctly. Injury, illness, and age are all possible reasons for hearing loss. However, the biggest controllable threat to your hearing is exposure to loud sounds for long periods of time. In the United States alone, it's estimated that between 10 million and 17 million people suffer from some form of hearing loss caused by excessive noise.

Why is noise pollution so dangerous? High-decibel sounds can place too much strain on the sensitive and delicate parts of the inner ear. When a noise is too loud, it begins to kill hair cells in the inner ear. The longer you are exposed to the loud noise, the more hair cells are destroyed. As the number of living hair cells decreases, so does your ability to hear.

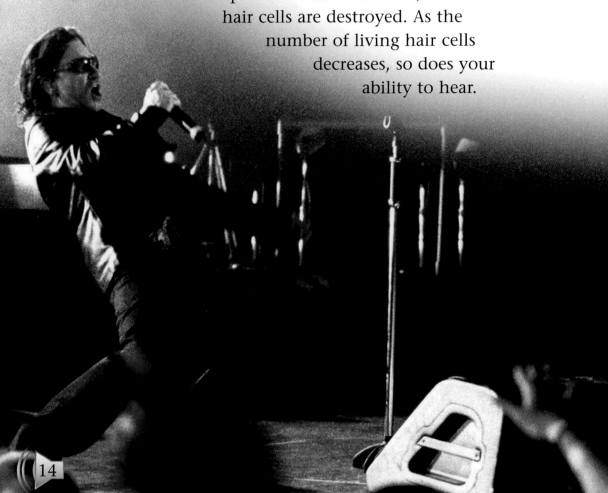

Over time, exposure to sound levels of 80 dB for 8 hours a day can cause **tinnitus**, a ringing, buzzing, or roaring sensation in the ears or head. Repeated exposure to sound levels higher than 80 dB can do even more damage.

Everyday items such as alarm clocks and stereos can create high levels of noise. Similarly, city traffic and garbage trucks have decibel levels that at best irritate your ears.

More frightening are the dangerous decibel levels at some movie theaters, concerts, and sporting events. Exposure to these extremely loud noises can cause long-term damage to your hearing. What's more, a sudden loud noise of 120 dB or higher can instantly cause permanent tinnitus or hearing loss.

Symptoms of Hearing Loss or Damage

- You experience ringing, tingling, or pain in one or both ears.
- Sounds seem to be muffled.
- Quiet sounds are hard or impossible to hear.
- One or both ears feels plugged.
- Your ability to hear seems to come and go.

Hearing aids can help people who have some hearing loss.

Amplified music at concerts can be extremely damaging to your hearing.

15

Protecting Your Ears

No one would advise a bicyclist to ride a bike without putting on a helmet. A soccer player wouldn't enter a match without pulling on shin guards. A smart skier would never zoom down a mountain without wearing goggles.

Yet, have you ever considered inserting earplugs before watching an explosive action thriller? Many high-tech movie sound systems can reach decibel levels of 85 dB and beyond. Two hours of exposure to that much noise is definitely not healthy for your hearing. However, chances are that you do not even own a pair of earplugs.

Airport workers are not allowed near the planes without ear protection.

Hearing loss may be the number one disability in the world. However, hearing loss and tinnitus caused by exposure to high-decibel sounds can be prevented. Here's what you can do and when to do it.

First, you should own earplugs. Earplugs are the easiest and most useful tool you can use to protect yourself against harmful noise. Usually made of foam or a gel-like form of silicone, earplugs are small inserts that fit snugly into the outer ear canal. They muffle, or reduce, noise before it reaches your inner ear.

Earplugs often come in different sizes, so it's important to choose a size that fits comfortably in your ear. Different kinds of earplugs also reduce different amounts of noise. In many areas of the world, earplugs have a Noise Reduction Rating (NRR) that gives you an idea of the number of decibels the earplugs filter from your ears. Earplugs with an NRR of 25, for example, reduce the amount of noise entering your inner ear by about 25 dB. When used correctly, many earplugs can reduce the amount of noise you hear by more than 30 dB.

If a noise is loud enough to make you feel uncomfortable, it can damage your hearing. Use earplugs, such as those shown here, or cover your ears to muffle the offending sound.

Another way to protect your hearing is to be aware of the harmful noises you encounter in your environment. For example, if you are going to a concert, think about how loud the musician or band is likely to be. (Many rock bands play at decibel levels of more than 100 dB.) Prepare by wearing your earplugs.

Also, consider the noise in your home. You'd be surprised at how loud a television, radio, vacuum cleaner, or other everyday household appliance can be. If you can't easily carry on a conversation with someone who's at least 3 feet away, it's likely that the sound levels in the room are at or above 85 dB.

Try to keep your television, stereo, and computer volumes at a low level. Avoid having too many noise-producing devices running at the same time. Finally, try to spend at least some time each day in a quiet space. By being aware of your surroundings and preparing for loud noises, you can help protect your hearing.

Common household appliances, such as blenders, can create noises that are so loud you have to shout to be heard over them.

Hazardous to Your Health

Loss of hearing is a big concern when it comes to noise. However, it certainly is not the only concern. A jet engine that drowns you out when you're talking on the telephone can annoy you. A faucet that drips all night can keep you awake. The drone of your upstairs neighbor's television can drive you crazy. These examples of noise may not threaten your hearing, but they can still have other damaging mental and physical effects, such as anxiety, depression, and headaches.

Can Noise Hurt Your Pet?

Noise isn't only harmful to human ears. It can have a negative effect on animals, too. In the wild, a loud noise can mask the sounds that animals use to hunt for prey, escape from predators, and communicate with one another. Short blasts of noise—from fireworks, for example—can frighten or panic both wild animals and pets. Even underwater noise caused by ship engines and sonar can be harmful to whales, porpoises, and other marine mammals.

Over time, exposure to loud noise can have the same result in many animals as it does in humans: hearing loss.

Finding a quiet place to do homework is important.

Noise can make you more irritable and less productive. Have you ever been studying in a noisy place and found that it was almost impossible to concentrate? Do you sometimes feel more frustrated or get angry with people around you in a noisy place? Believe it or not, some of your reactions may have come from your noisy surroundings.

It is important to have quiet time each day in order to rest, listen to soft music, or study. Remember that sounds are directed through your ears and into your brain through nerve endings. Too much noise can overwhelm your brain by causing you to try to focus on too many things at once. Spending time in a quiet environment is an important way to give your brain a rest.

Noise in the Workplace

Some people have jobs that expose them to unhealthy levels of sound. Over the years, airport workers, carpenters and construction workers, factory workers, miners, truck drivers, trash collectors, and others can develop hearing and health problems caused by noise. Safety standards require many employers to provide ear protection to use in the workplace. However, it is the responsibility of each worker to actually use the safety equipment.

This worker protects his ears while using a chain saw.

Studies have shown that noise may be linked to many different health problems. People exposed to constant sources of noise pollution report more headaches, insomnia, accidents, and anxiety. Exposure to long periods of noise over time can cause problems related to heart rate, blood pressure, and digestion. It can cause exhaustion as well.

Noise can make us tense and angry. Some studies have shown a link between noise pollution and increased aggression or depression. Knowing that noise can affect your health may motivate you to find ways to guard against its more damaging effects.

A dripping faucet is well known for being an irritating noise and can cause stress levels to increase!

Noise Pollution: A Growing Concern

Noise in the environment comes from many different sources. Sometimes we add noise to the environment ourselves, such as when we operate noisy appliances or equipment. At other times, we experience noise that comes from someone or something out of our control.

The fact that someone else produces a noise doesn't make it any less damaging. Just as second-hand smoke can harm us and pollute the air, second-hand noise can also negatively affect our bodies and our environment. Noise pollution cannot be seen. It does not leave a visible trace, such as a smoky haze over a city. Noise pollution is also hard to measure. It can come and go with the single blast of a horn. Yet its negative effects are beyond doubt.

Jet-skiing can be fun, but its loud buzzing sound can scare away wildlife as well as annoy people.

Noise pollution is a major and growing concern in both urban and suburban population centers. Over the past one hundred years, noise pollution has steadily increased with the growth of cities. However, noise pollution can also affect any wilderness area that is in the flight path of a jumbo jet. High-pitched, loud, and many different overlapping sounds all contribute to noise pollution. Indoors, appliances hum, fans rattle, clocks tick, boards creak, and water drips. Outdoors, it can be hard to escape the noise from traffic, construction equipment, pets, and the general roar of everyday life.

Noise Over the Years

Noise is not a new complaint. More than 2,300 years ago in the ancient city of Sybaris, in what is now southern Italy, laws were passed to reduce noise. Over the last few centuries, as development and the use of machinery has increased, so has noise pollution. This trend is expected to continue as populations increase worldwide.

This photo shows a factory worker in 1923 using a drop-forging hammer, a noisy piece of machinery.

For years, noise pollution had been considered more of a nuisance than a hazard. Research has made clear its dangers only recently. As a result, efforts are being made—especially in urban settings—to cut down on certain types of noise pollution. Airports have adjusted flight patterns to reduce the number of airplanes that fly over areas where many people live. Barriers have been built between highways and residential areas to cut down on traffic noise. Local governments have passed laws, or ordinances, limiting the use of leaf blowers, jackhammers, and other gardening and construction equipment to certain times of the day. Some vehicles have been modified to run more quietly.

The fuel-cell automobile is a recent development in the fight against noise pollution. The car is powered by hydrogen, not gasoline, and it is noise- and pollution-free.

Noise: It's Against the Law!

Local governments around the world have passed laws designed to quieten their communities. Here are just a few examples:

- Drivers can be fined in some places if the music from their car stereos is too loud.
- A neighbor heard fighting and screaming can be arrested, fined, and jailed.
- The owner of a dog left outside to howl at the Moon all night can be fined or jailed.
- Many towns forbid owning roosters. Even if a town allows roosters, the law may limit the number that can be owned.

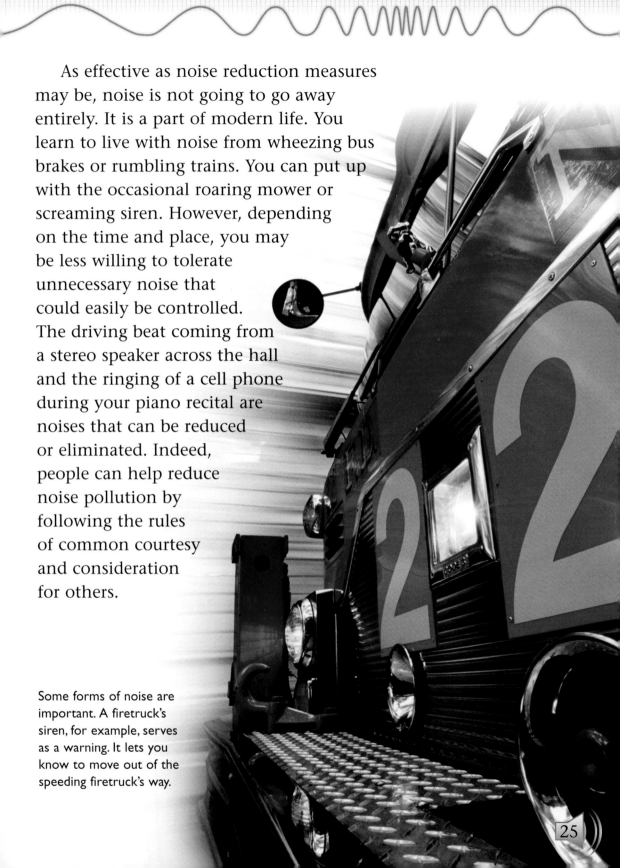

As effective as noise reduction measures may be, noise is not going to go away entirely. It is a part of modern life. You learn to live with noise from wheezing bus brakes or rumbling trains. You can put up with the occasional roaring mower or screaming siren. However, depending on the time and place, you may be less willing to tolerate unnecessary noise that could easily be controlled. The driving beat coming from a stereo speaker across the hall and the ringing of a cell phone during your piano recital are noises that can be reduced or eliminated. Indeed, people can help reduce noise pollution by following the rules of common courtesy and consideration for others.

Some forms of noise are important. A firetruck's siren, for example, serves as a warning. It lets you know to move out of the speeding firetruck's way.

Fighting Back Against Noise

Around the world, the message that noise pollution can be dangerous is being heard loud and clear. Many organizations are focusing their energy on raising awareness about the problems of noise pollution and promoting hearing health. Here's just a small sample of what concerned people are doing to fight against noise.

Noise Action Day

Each June, people in the United Kingdom band together to fight noise on Noise Action Day. Organized by the National Society for Clean Air, a British environmental group, Noise Action Day is designed to encourage people to come up with simple solutions to noise problems. Many communities sponsor school programs about noise and hearing and civic programs about noise pollution control.

Teachers and pupils in Cardiff, Wales, turn out to support Noise Action Day.

Farm Noise and Hearing Project

The Farm Noise and Hearing Network recognizes that noise pollution is becoming more and more common in rural areas. The organization is made up of farmers and health care professionals from southern Australia. It sponsors the Farm Noise and Hearing Project, a campaign designed to educate residents of southern Australian rural communities about the dangers of noise.

Field days let farmers learn how to protect their hearing.

According to the organization, 60 to 80 percent of farmers between the ages of thirty and seventy have suffered hearing loss caused by exposure to farm machinery. The project aims to reduce that number by making farmers aware of the dangers of loud farm noise. Members of the Farm Noise and Hearing Project sponsor field days and health events throughout southern Australia. They test farmers' hearing and give advice about ways that farmers can protect themselves from the dangers of noise.

This noisy combine harvester can make farmwork a danger to hearing health.

Hearing Education and Awareness for Rockers (H.E.A.R.)

Fifteen out of every thousand people under the age of eighteen have some form of hearing loss. Approximately 60 percent of those inducted into the Rock and Roll Hall of Fame in Cleveland, Ohio, have impaired hearing. H.E.A.R. is a nonprofit group based in the United States. It was started by Kathy Peck, a rock musician who suffered hearing damage after performing in a concert in 1984. H.E.A.R. promotes information on hearing and hearing protection for musicians and music lovers. Members produce programs for school students and record television and radio public service announcements to raise awareness of the risks that amplified music poses to artists and fans.

From a distance of 4 to 6 feet, amplified rock music measures approximately 120 dB.

What You Can Do

Regulations that keep certain sources of noise pollution under control cannot completely restore peace and quiet to the world, nor can these regulations prevent all hearing loss. Individuals must do their part to keep things quiet, too. What can you do about noise pollution?

- Be aware of the noise you create. For example, keep the volume low on your stereo, television, and computer.
- Respect places in which calm and quiet are important, such as libraries, places of worship, restaurants, and theaters.
- If you own a cell phone, turn it off or set it to vibrate before entering quiet places. Remind your family members and friends to do the same thing.
- Learn all you can about noise pollution and help educate your friends and family about its dangers.

Your cell phone can be disruptive in places such as restaurants and libraries.

Other people's musical tastes may not be the same as yours—so keep it low.

Keep quiet in places such as libraries where any noise can disturb others.

Are You Listening?

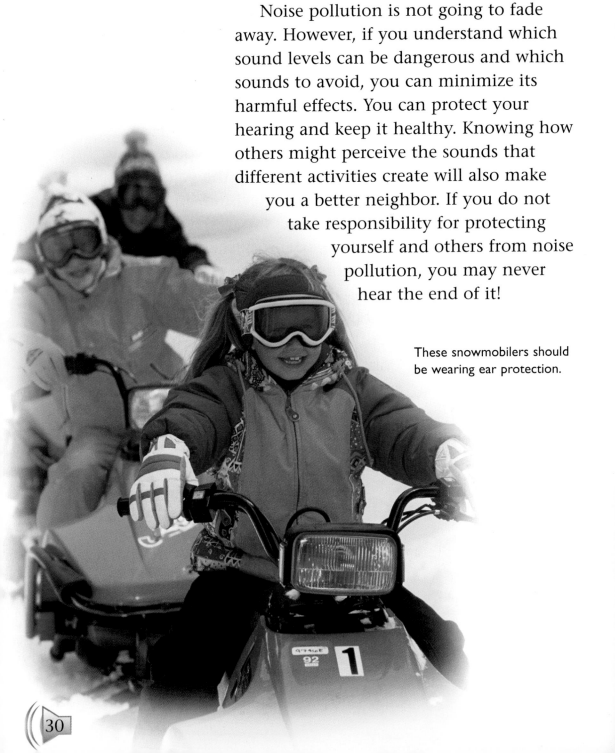

Noise pollution is not going to fade away. However, if you understand which sound levels can be dangerous and which sounds to avoid, you can minimize its harmful effects. You can protect your hearing and keep it healthy. Knowing how others might perceive the sounds that different activities create will also make you a better neighbor. If you do not take responsibility for protecting yourself and others from noise pollution, you may never hear the end of it!

These snowmobilers should be wearing ear protection.

Glossary

absorb   take in sound without reflecting it

amplify   make a sound stronger

amplitude   the height of the crests of a sound wave; related to the loudness, or intensity, of a sound

compressed   squeezed together

crest   the highest point of a wave

decibels   units used to measure the relative loudness of sounds

noise   unwanted sound

noise pollution annoying or harmful noise in an environment

reflection   sound that is turned or thrown back

sound waves   alternating low and high pressure vibrations that move through matter and are interpreted as sound when collected in the ear

tinnitus   ringing or buzzing in the ears

trough   the lowest point of a wave

vibrates   moves back and forth very quickly

Index